Heart to Heart 2

Heart to Heart 2

Love, Loss and Healing

PENE ENOCHS

© 2017 Pene Enochs
All rights reserved.

ISBN: 069280286X
ISBN 13: 9780692802861

"Life is a song - sing it.
Life is a game - play it.
Life is a challenge -meet it.
Life is a dream - realize it.
Life is a sacrifice - offer it.
Life is love - enjoy it. "

SAI BABA

Dedicated
To
My Friend

Bill

"In the sweetness of friendship
let there be laughter,
and sharing of pleasures.
For in the dew of little things the heart
finds its morning and is refreshed."

KHALIL GIBRAN

Contents

Acknowledgement · xv
Forward · xvii

Part 1   Continuation of Life · · · · · · · · · · · · · · · · · · · 1
One · 3
        My Life Goes On · 3
        My Solace · 7
Two · 10
        Ellen · 10
        Bill · 15
        Butterfly · 17
Three · 20
        My Angel in Disguise · · · · · · · · · · · · · · · · · · 20
        Mission · 24
        My Unending Love · 26
        Unconditional Love · 29

Part 2   Love And Loss · 31
Four · 33

	Love · 33	
	Divine Love · 34	
Part 3	The Healing · 39	
Five · 41
	Loss And Healing · 41
	Embrace and Release · · · · · · · · · · · · · · · · · 45
Six · 47
	The Illness · 47
	My Story · 51
Seven · 54
	Crohn's Disease · 56
	Road to Recovery · 60
Part 4	On A Lighter Side · 67
Eight · 69
	Single and a Senior Citizen · · · · · · · · · · · · · 69
	Just Me · 72
Nine · 75
	Hearts Touching · 75
	Tom · 77
Ten · 82
	Entering the Ballroom · · · · · · · · · · · · · · · · · 82
	Exuberant Contacts · · · · · · · · · · · · · · · · · · · 85
	Butterfly Dance · 86
Eleven · 88
	Dancing Around the Chair · · · · · · · · · · · · · 88
	The Montana Band · · · · · · · · · · · · · · · · · · · 89

Twelve		94
	The Journey Continue	94
	Fleeting Connections	98
	Last Dance	103
Thirteen		106
	Playing It Forward	106
	My Little Book	110
Part 5	My Persecutive	113
Fourteen		115
	Transformation	115
	Our Survival	118
Fifteen		120
	Food for Thought	120
	A New Day	126

Acknowledgement

Much gratitude to Clark, for his tenaciousness in editing my book. I'm ever so thankful that he did not give up on me.

To my Sheila "Doll" who has been along on my new journey. Thank you for your support, time and effort. Your encouragement and friendship is one of my treasured Gifts.

Also, to the ones in my book, I am so thankful that I met you, and you became a part of my life. For without you, this book would've never been written.

Another one of my Post Scripts, there are so many people that I could not put in my book, nonetheless, you are all special to me. Without the friendship of my "Dancing Buds" my life would not have been so full of love and laughter. To all who touched my life, I give you thanks and my Unconditional Love.

Forward

After having a life changing experience a couple years back while encountering a chance meeting with my Twin Flame, Soul Mate, Old Soul or whatever description inferred; had left my life in disarray. Trying to make peace within myself, seemed to be a big job. Disengaging from old conceptions of tribal moldings, religious dogma, internal and external influences was daunting, to say the least. Trying to bring together some semblance of normalcy seemed at best, remote. While within this world of duality, there was emerging, a new consciousness. While searching within, I found myself. With this significant self-awareness came self-love, and healing. After many years of searching for happiness and joy, I was finally home, within myself. Believing that a certain person or persons could make me happy was no longer a yearning or need. All my happiness was deep inside, ready to be reborn.

Existing within these two worlds has been an on-going experience. Being in the very heart of the matter, is where life truly begins. For the ones like me, there is a new life in transition. It was like opening a new door, leading into wonderful new experiences, places and people. My world has been turned upside down, wrong side out, and made anew. Breaking away from outmoded precepts and preconditions, has placed me in a state of an awakening of love, loss and healing. Believing not only from my own perspective, but also of worldly matters. That of being in a healing and transitional period. Seeing with a new awareness, has once more been transforming.

My life continues changing every day in all areas of my life. Let me say from the very first, that every experience has not been easy. There has been that darker side. Living in this world of transition has many obstacles; and this new beginning at my very core is primal. At these new beginnings, there are so many physical and mental changes within the body. Even as an aspirant in an unfamiliar arena; life continues to be exciting and challenging.

My entire life has been full of challenges. a major part filled with illness and personal tragedies. however, with faith and endurance, my life continues to transform.

On a lighter side, it seems, my new world is ongoing with special individuals; that have touched my heart and soul. The interactions of these special people, each in their own unique way, have made my life easier and more joyful. Touching lightly on these stories, while the real focus lay in the transforming of love, loss and healing.

Through God's amazing grace and *unconditional love* for us, makes *healing* a possibility.

> "It was the best of times,
> it was the worst of times,
> it was the age of wisdom,
> it was the age of foolishness,
> it was the epoch of belief,
> it was the epoch of incredulity,
> it was the season of Light,
> it was the season of Darkness,
> it was the spring of hope,
> it was the winter of despair,
> we had everything before us,
> we had nothing before us."

CHARLES DICKENS' A TALE OF TWO CITIES

Heart to Heart 2

"The key to growth is the introduction of higher dimensions of consciousness into our awareness."

LAO TZU

Part 1
Continuation of Life

Pene Enochs

There exists only the present instant...
a Now which always and without end is itself new.
There is no yesterday nor any tomorrow, but only
Now as it was a thousand years ago and as
it will be a thousand years hence.

MEISTER ECKHART

One

"Life is a series of a natural and
spontaneous changes.
Don't resist them – that it only creates sorrow.
Let reality be reality.
Let things flow naturally forward
In whatever way, they like"

Lao Tzu

MY LIFE GOES ON

It seems my life continues a roller coaster existence. Going from having a heart to heart, soul to soul encounter with the most incredible man, to another loss of my dearest friend. My life appears to be that of a caterpillar; metamorphosing in unknown ways. In one minute, I find myself in the deepest unimaginable love, and in the next transforming moment I find myself changing to that of deep despair. Nonetheless, my life is continually transforming into a renewed presence.

What a paradox! Of course, when getting back into reality, I realized this phenomenon was transient, and basically just another life lesson. We know that all emotions are experienced by everyone. In one way or the other, how we respond and react to these challenges, are by our own choosing.

My mind is racing through thoughts of the past few years, and I am in awe. It seems my love, loss, and healing is an ongoing process. In my previous book, Heart to Heart, a gift of unconditional love, it was truly just that, a miraculous gift of unconditional love. Unconditional love has changed my entire way of looking and living at life. Giving of this amazing love to everyone has been ongoing. With a word, a smile, or a touch, it appears this love is overflowing, and to be given freely. It is so easy to smile, to give encouragement, or simply the healing touch of a hug.

Recap
In the following chapters, I recap my experience with my Angel, my cousin Ellen, my dear friend Bill; and several new people that have touched my life in such profound and endearing ways. I am blessed to have met such wonderful human beings.

In my journey of love, loss and healing, I go back in time to a place where I was given a true miracle. My story, may be too graphic for some; nonetheless, this is my story.

It appears my life has always been surrounded by many of these "*accidental*" circumstances. I am the recipient of *providential* intervention in so many areas of my life, and thus, it is a continuing force. Some of my stories are of love, divine love, while some contain stories of loss; and of recovery, that of healing.

A NEW DAY

Each day has its challenges. The waves of time affecting each consequential course of action, shaded with its innumerable trials. Even with these new spiritual beginnings, life still faces the confrontation of simply living in the current reality. Although at times, intervals of uncertainty emerge and demand a presence. All the while trying to change lifelong moldings of characteristics and beliefs. These new changes appear to be at times, an overwhelming task. With a new conscious awareness, I am ready and eager to begin a new way of living. Changes within my present cognition, bring an awareness of the importance of another day. Even with this wellspring of love and loss, once again there is a continual search in finding my innermost self.

After another year of ever changing events, the reconstruction of my life continues. With a new awareness, life would be simpler. However, finding that person within is challenging. With the help of Stuart Wilde's video, "Infinite Self: 33 Steps to Reclaiming Your Inner Power," slowly but surely, it is as though my life has finally found its predestined path.

Every day in this space of time, there is a continuous changing of mind and body. With our minds and hearts projected toward that divine relationship with God, gives us the real reason for living. We are striving to fill that interspace, so that it might bring us closer to enlightenment. A continual metamorphosis of the spiritual self and body is transforming.

MY SOLACE

   While sitting on my porch, and looking out over the landscape, I find myself absorbing natures tranquilizer. Such a blessing, and right here in my backyard. Thinking of the days gone by, my thoughts are brought into a moment of yesterday. While looking for a new home, my husband stumbled upon this one. Thinking to myself, this house was certainly out of our price range. However, "*providence*" seems to intervene, in the most opportune moment; and it appears this is where we belong. This home was everything, happy, joyful; and a wonderful place to raise our twin girls. Little did I know at the time; this back porch would become my solace in later years.

As I sit on my back porch enjoying nature's wonderment, not only am I in awe of the magnificent view, but of all the wild and wonderful creatures therein. If this alone was not enough, the most spectacular occurrence happens in the evening. For then I am witness to the most glorious sunsets, appearing right before my eyes. Unbelievable colors of magenta, orange, yellow and gold; seemingly fashioned by an unknown artist's hand.

For if perchance I had to make recompense for this wonderful experience, my coffers would become empty, and likewise, I would become a pauper. So therefore, my pittance, my mere payment of gratitude is bestowed upon this tiny parcel of nature, just beyond my porch.

"When you are joyous, look deep into your heart and you shall find it is only that which has given you sorrow that is giving you joy.
When you are sorrowful look again in your heart, and you shall see that in truth you are weeping for that which has been your delight."

KHALIL GIBRAN

Two

"Goodbyes are only for those who love with their eyes.
Because for those who love with their heart and soul
There is no such thing as separation."

Rumi

ELLEN

My dear cousin Ellen, is still a big factor in my life. Although, not in a bodily sense; nonetheless, she remains a big factor in my well-being. Without the virtual highway of cyberspace communication, there would be little interaction. In the progression of intercommunication, with merely a thought, can bring her to me in a moment's notice. She is always available, helpful and mindful of my wellbeing. (I'm so glad she's in my gene pool)

Without the daily comfort of my confidant, my little mother, my dear cousin; I am left with a loss of sorts. With everything, there seems to be that duality, always present in underlying tones. She is with me spiritually, but not in my physical world. When asking myself, what lesson can be created out of this separation? Apparently, the main reason being, is to push myself out of my safety zone, and to learn how to nurture the lonely child within.

Homeward Bound
Ellen has return home to care for her ailing brother. Her demeanor may appear slightly fragile, but inside lives a veritable tiger. Her protective nature carries over in all aspects of her life. Being my rock and support in this past year was virtually invaluable to my well-being. Not only did she care for me physically when I had broken my hip, but she was there every minute to lift me up mentally.

Now, she is caring for my cousin Steve who is in the final stage of cancer. She is his strength and rock to lean on, until his final breath.

The loss of not having Ellen daily in my life, has been another one of those lessons. Finding within myself the ability to take another step, as another healing begins.

On the Road Again
On a much lighter side, I feel the need to recap an experience with my dear Ellen. This is just another little story

about our travels. It seems all our traveling experiences end up being just that....an ongoing experience. The moment we enter my little blue Prius, the adventures seem to begin. Not quite understanding why this happens, but knowing the energy we two exude, seems to magnetize the frivolity gene within us. Which I guess that, answers my own question.

The morning has arrived; and we are on our way to Kerrville, a small city in Texas. One of my yearly visits to see my son Dean. This may seem to some, as a little drive in the hill country. However, our little jaunts on the road have never been the ordinary driving experience. These meanderings have taken us far and wide, and to areas unknown. Most of our journeys are usually short in mileage, nevertheless, the extent of time it takes warrants a longer predominance. It most certainly is in our behalf, never to be in a hurry! For some unknown reason, our trips seem to take on a life of their own. Even though all kinds of travel devices are at our disposal, nonetheless, our past miscarriages continue to plague us. As a copilot of sorts, reading signs, maps and even with the help of a GPS, it appears my perceivable intuition becomes null and void in the area of navigation. It still amazes me to the fact that I've ridden on these roads many times, yet the moment Ellen and I begin our excursion, some unforeseen circumstance emerges.

I need to make a disclaimer at this point. The times of being lost, may have seemingly made me appear to be a little crazy and ruffled at some point. However, most of the times when lost or simply off the beaten path, we have discovered wonderful new sights and places. So, the time factor plays a secondary role in our adventures. We have learned to be open and obliging to this element in our travels.

Arriving at our destination may take a bit longer, due to the fact, that we may have missed the road. (Once again, I must take the heat; for Ellen remains clueless). Nevertheless, we are becoming very familiar with the area. Hence, taking advantage, and making time for a little respite, in our new venue.

Now, we are on our way, without delay to our destination; and adding only a mere hour to our time schedule. Perhaps you are thinking, that these are isolated incidents in the perils of Ellen and Pene. Ahem, NOT! Our adventures are continually materializing in our lives. Most likely because we are open and flexible to *"providence."*

A little note about Ellen, after my hip surgery; my friend Earl, took Ellen, baggage and I up to the Texas Panhandle. Ellen and I were the collaborators on this venture. Although, it seems we may have been a bad influence on Earl's navigation. Before getting to our main destination, it seems we have maneuvered into a dead-end zone. Our excursion has led us into an industrial area; with many circled dead-end roads. With much laughter, and without further help from Ellen and I, Earl finally found his way to the main highway. We were on our way to our destination, without any other distraction or problems from the inert passengers.

Another LITTLE NOTE: Ellen and I are contemplating a road trip in the summer. Since I am the notorious map reader/ navigator; prayer requests are coveted!

Changes

After almost a year, my life continues to change, as in the life of a butterfly. It appears those in my life that are important to me, arrive at the right time and then exit on cue. There are times when it is hard for me to grasp the reality of the moment. Even with the desire of wanting and needing certain people in my life, there appears to come a time of dissolution. All in all, just another one of those *"seasons of my life."*

Once more, I find myself in this "theater of life." My dear cousin has found her new life renewed with her family, for there she is the most needed. I am so fortunate that she has touched my life after these many years, but now I must surrender once again, another person in my life. Hence, the continuing journey of my life is ever flowing.

BILL

A little note about my friend Bill, yes, we have remained friends! On my last visit, there hasn't been too big a change. However, on a recent visit to his home in Houston, again I am at a disadvantage. I inherently know that I should never touch the TV controls, least I find myself again without navigational tools. (as well we know, my navigational skills are limited). Here I am once more, in a house full of unfamiliar electronic appliances and gadgets. While sitting on the couch reading, I reach over to turn the lamp on. OK NOW....how do I turn this lamp on? Using all my initiative simply to have light, it seems darkness is remaining in my reality. With the creativity of my friend, it seems he has programed all the light switches to his command. Not only do the lamps, lights and everything electronically answer to his touch; but even his refrigerator, that refuses to obey my request for simply a glass of water.

As I had previously mentioned before, Bill and I appear to be the odd couple/friends. The bottom line being, despite our differences, we still have remained friends over these many years.

Post Script

I have yet another impending loss before me. It appears my dearest friend has been diagnosed with pancreatic cancer. His disease has progressed to his lungs and brain, leaving him very debilitated. My mind is once again in constant motion. I have suffered the loss of my son Mark, my best friend, Edna, my husband Billy, and friend Sandy, just over these recent years. Once more, I am devastated beyond words. My journey has taken me once again into a new and unknown direction. In my mind, the changes to my life are insurmountable and unbelievable. My sobs, tears, and grief have encompassed my being. That first stage begins, one of disbelief. Having Bill in my life for almost 20 years, and suddenly realizing that he will no longer be there for me, leaves an unimaginable void within my heart. No longer will we sit on that infamous deck with our IPads, no face-timing, no mentoring of electronic gadgets, no more advice, and no more being able to see my dear friend, face to face.

I am at a loss! However, knowing there is a time allotted for each one, and it is the inevitable for all of us. We must embrace the time that allowed us to become friends, and relish the memories. Then we must release, release that person that bonded with us for so many years. Knowing, the healing process can begin once we release these emotions of ones we have loved so dearly. I have been truly blessed, with my heart to heart connection with my friend, Bill. God may be calling him home, but he has allowed me to relish and relive memories of days gone by. Like the caterpillar, we are all in a metamorphosis, forever changing.

BUTTERFLY

As the Caterpillar begins its metamorphosis;
the little butterfly-self is emerging and transforming.
Miraculously, the layers of the old self are being
rent in the prevailing moments....
Wearing a way of outmoded concepts, bonds
of fearfulness, and negativity.
Deep within the pupae lay the reawakening
of a renewed spirit.
This diminutive creature of a new beginning,
has begun a new virginal experience of evolution.
Changing from the old to the new by
means of rebirthing is to induce a new beginning.
No aforethought to the past of
regulations, mores, codes or moldings;
but now leading this unique entity to a new awareness.
As in the layers of an onion
each thickness is peeled away,
one mantle at a time; and within emerges the
presence of something brand new.
At first glance, the appearance seems to be
evolving slowly, yet remains diligent.
Moving and turning, as if in the birthing canal.
Unmistakably, knowing the effort spent is to come alive;
after this long sleep.
Standing alone and with trembling wings,

she has come alive.
With renewed vigor, she begins her quest to
follow her heart,
and to be what she was created for.
This beautiful transforming miracle from God....
the BUTTERFLY

PENE

"It is only with the heart that one can see rightly; what is essential is invisible to the eye."

ANTOINE DE SAINT-EXUPERY

Three

"The meeting of two personalities is like the contact of two chemical substances; if there is any reaction both are transformed."

C.G. JUNG

MY ANGEL IN DISGUISE

I have lived these many years, and have never met or touched that special person that could complete my life, until now. In that first embrace, it appears my life really mattered. It seemed that I had been given a miraculous gift from God. This overwhelming Divine Unconditional Love has given me the ability to love another with every facet of my being.

Connecting heart-to-heart with another human being at any age and on any level, can be compelling to say the least. Such a credulous event occurring in my run of the mill life, brought about intense, and unfamiliar emotions. When such an unsuspecting miracle occurs in such an ordinary life, the change can seem extraordinary and unreal. My mind and heart released all-powerful mixed emotions and feelings that apparently have never been valued or experienced up to this point in my life. Without exception, every emotion presented itself in various ways and circumstances; impassioned with inconceivable and unbelievable feelings at the moment of conception.

In Retrospect

After having been given this all-consuming, miraculous gift of unconditional love. I asked myself WHY? My questioning mind prevailed once again. However, knowing full well the answers are within my own mind. In this shell of humanness exists an undying, magnanimous, embodiment of spiritual love and joy. Despite my inward spiritual voice's direction, outwardly my heart desires that earthly relationship. A duality of sorts is intimated. While my heart desired earthly matters, my spirit-man dictates primary metaphysical directives.

Believing that I'm expected to give this Divine Unconditional Love back to others, my heart beats with uncertainty. It seems this divine gift of love from God was not meant for an earthly relationship. The touching of two hearts brought about intense love vibrating on a higher level.

Energies

The touching of my Heart to Heart connection internalizes a bond of energy; unlike anything I've ever experienced.

Within this embodiment of carbon based elements resides a spiritual, ethereal soul. The vibratory experience of this emotion expounds upon its very existence. It creates a frequency of energy, like a song invading my consciousness. Like a heavenly melody played in varying cadences. A small mingling of energetic pulsation is always present. Then there are times in which a crescendo of a strong vibrational rhythm is felt. There are sensations that seem to encompass my entire being energetically, and appears at different intervals of time. Through these vibrations and unconditional love my prayers and meditations are directed to every living thing on this planet. Love and light permeating my very soul, is my gift to be given back into this earthly reality. Therefore, this amazing gift of Unconditional Love, is truly the existence of my being. It appears now, this is my mission in life.

In due season, through endurance and sought out patience, time has brought me to a place of emancipation. Release has not been an easy journey. These earthly desires seem to rise up and want preoccupation over spiritual direction. When seeking answers, the arrival of solutions miraculously appears at a pre-ordained time. Perhaps not as I had hoped for, but solutions nonetheless. Living day by day in absolution, may not be as I had envisioned, but with God's help, his will be done.

My Surrender

Having very little knowledge of metaphysical theories or beliefs, yet I find myself amid the phenomenon of twin flames. The meeting of a twin flame is unexpected and life changing. There is an instant recognition, a feeling of being safe and home. Some twins are meant to have relationships on the earth, while others are meant only to connect and come together for a purpose or mission. Each connection is unique and different. There appears to be 8 stages in the twin flames experience. Surrender is based on one of these steps.

I know within my heart and soul, that I have been blessed with this unique connection, has revealed to me that I must give this unconditional love back into a world in need of love and light. Having lived through the pain of such highly explosive emotions, it appears my road to recovery is in sight. Experiencing such an intense relationship for a brief moment was the citadel for Divine Love. As the intensity of such emotions embody my entire being, it is a hard thing to do, to surrender.

Knowing this phenomenon is merely a tiny happening among the cosmos. Cause and purpose seem to be played out in this arena of life. In my state of love and surrender; the mere act of giving up something so dear and precious is heart wrenching. When given this true gift of Unconditional Love, one would expect it to be everlasting. Everlasting it is, however not in this dimensional life. In this life, purpose outweighs earthly embodiment. Therefore, adhering to the will of God is the reason for existence. Our presence at this place in time is by His will and purpose for us. Giving back the very thing that God has given us, that of Unconditional Love, is the purpose for this experience. The evolution of this Divine Unconditional Love has been ongoing. it evolves from primal beginnings, and finally arrives to this ultimate state of spiritual/ethereal love.

MISSION

Duality plays the final chapter in the scheme of things. With intense divine love comes the element of the egoic shadow self. When Unconditional Divine Love enters the very core of this human vessel, comprehension is unexplainable and indescribable. Receiving this intense love is in a higher realm and given to this earthly being, for purpose. Within this powerful love comes the duality of pain and ecstasy. While through this gamut of massive emotions, reality sets in....the mission!

Having to forfeit, give up, surrender, that very spark within your soul, is beyond pain. However, while vacillating in between this world of duality, a solution emanates. With this amazing God-given gift, self-realization of purposeful meaning is ever evolving. Giving up oneself is the beginning of one's healing. Only when we give back to God, what He has richly given to us, can we begin to heal. Being continually mindful of the circumstances of others and the care of our living planet; a healing can be promoted.

RECONCILIATION

Through meditation and prayers, I have been led on this emotional pathway into my purpose for being. In knowing that this is my lot in life, I put my heart and soul into the release of everyone and everything that is bound to me. Going back to the loss of my husband, son and friends, and striving to give back what is expected of me. When we surrender our all to God, we are truly at one with him.

Finally, after surrendering everything that was blocking me, my life began turning around. It seemed that when releasing these emotions, it brought about my healing process. Unconditional love, was the product of these emotions. The total consuming power of unconditional love was the phenomenon of this uniting. Being able to form and mold this connection into a viable means of expressing oneself was the primary purpose of this union.

It appears we all have roles to play in this garden of life. Confirming in whatever belief one might have pertaining to life's involvement; we thrust forth to carry out our designated callings. In the final hour, we await the new millennium. In God's timing, our destiny awaits.

MY UNENDING LOVE

Some things are just meant to be.
You have touched the very center of my being,
within the dwelling place where my heart resides.
My very existence is changed merely
by your presence.
My thoughts of Eternal and Divine Love are
in continual motion,
ever evolving to that higher dimension.
My lips cannot begin to utter mere words of this
emotional profound love. There aren't words to
express this level of my adoration.
It is as though every cell in my body reacts
not only by a touch, but by the very
sound of your name. Activating those deep,
perhaps sleeping emotions once again.
In my thoughts, I find it so amazing to look
into your face, your eyes; and not only do I see
YOU...but I see ME!
I react not only to that look, but to the enfoldment
of my soul and spirit into you.
How can that be?....How can that be?
I love, you love, but when finding oneself in the
throes of an indescribable and unimaginable love;
it is beyond words.
When having this all-encompassing love for you,
it is on another level.

Perhaps in another reality or even another dimension.
Who can really know.
All we know is what resides within our hearts,
by a mere thought or action.
Wondering where that might've come from,
but realizing they may be memories
of long past. Forgotten memories, that are
brought forth into our earthly reality.
Stirring our memories and emotions, while looking in
our *in-most mirror*, we can recognize our purpose.
Together, we can make a difference in our world.
Our love permeates the very air we breathe; knowing that Love,
is truly the answer to all our problems on this earth.
Here we find ourselves in the transformation of evolution.
By our own choosing, we dedicate ourselves
to our mission of love.
Even though we are apart, we are still connected.
The path that I go down may not be the
path that you're following; however,
through the bond of Divine Love, we persevere.
We love, because we
have been loved, we continue to love,
and we have love everlasting.
What an overwhelming thought!
Love in any form is powerful.
There are so many ways we love and are loved;
Like Elizabeth Barrett Browning stated,
"let me count the ways."

I love you because you are you,
I love you because you are a part of me,
I love you because of your spirit,
I love you because of your existence,
I love that you are real to me; and
I love that you love me.
I love you as real as our illusions can be.
Is all an illusion on this earth?
Are we merely holograms that have spirit and a soul?
How can that be?
Yet we know that we are earthly and expend energies,
and we know our energies attract other like energies.
Just as we are connected....by our very
own unique vibration.
That's a miracle to me!
Loving you so dearly, has brought me
to this hour in time.
We give our lives over to the universal
wisdom Of God's will.
Continuing our paths to that state of higher being,
made possible by this beautiful eternal truth of Love.
We are made of love, love we are,
we have become love,
and we will remain in Love....Unending."

PENE

UNCONDITIONAL LOVE

"You are the very life within me,
you are cause of very breath I take.
I live because you live. I love because you love.
I belong to you and you alone.
You have my heart, my soul, my life in your hands.
We are bound together in this life and the next.
I love you unconditionally.... forever."

PENE

Part 2
Love And Loss

"Love is life, all that I understand.
I understand only because I love."

TOLSTOY

Four

> "It isn't impossible to love in part,
> you will wish that it was.
> You can transmute love, ignore it, muddle it,
> but you can never pull it out of you.
> I know by experience, that the poets are right;
> love is Eternal."
>
> E.M. FORSTER

LOVE

Love, is an immutable emotion. The definition of love garners feelings from adoration to wonderment. In this earthly sense to love comes easily, we may love that endeared person, our family, an animal, apple pie, or any other quintessential longing. Each presence recognizes a different element of love. With adoration, liking, and affection, we give ourselves totally to these feelings of passion.

A mere couple of weeks after the miracle of conception, the heart is the first organ to develop. Even our brain is secondary to the heart. The ability to love, stems from within the heart center. Taking this into consideration, it is no wonder that love is so important and vital to our welfare.

DIVINE LOVE

Definition of divine love has many different variations, as in the earthly love. A love that changes your entire life, within moments, is miraculous in itself. Transcendental, ethereal, spiritual, wonderful; there are no words to accurately describe this phenomenal experience of *"Divine Love."* The real definition of agape love comes from our Creator. God's love is Unconditional, Divine, and transcending to mankind. There has been much written about these four little letters, LO V E. Poets, authors, and songwriters have expounded upon this emotion from our very beginnings. I believe that love is the most powerful emotion that we, as human beings have been given. Loving and being loved is paramount in any society.

We know when nurturing and love is absent in a newborn; its very survival is in question. Even in the wildest kingdom, an emotional connection is made to the smallest animal. Taking a step farther, when witnessing different animals caring for other species of a different genus, it is truly amazing.

We cannot dismiss this wonderful plan of nature and existence on this planet.

I cannot help but wonder about the human species, it appears we have lost something in the past ages. Are we not higher than the animal kingdom? Have we not been given a spirit and soul? What of our humanity? Are we merely "robots" without sensitivity, intention or mission? Perhaps now is the time for us to re-evaluate what is true and worthwhile in this life. Looking within, and discovering the truth, can change us. We can make an impact and difference in this place we call "*home.*"

Since our creation began with Love, God's Unconditional Love; now it's time for us to return the gift. Give of our unconditional love to family, friends, neighbors, strangers and to those that may not even want our love. God loved us so much that he presented himself as the Christ persona, a perfect example for us. We have the choice, to be like Christ, the embodiment of love, or not. It is time for us to wake up and smell the roses, if we go don't one day our species will not be here to smell the flowers.

Origins of this Divine Love begins with God. God is unconditional love epitomized. This Eternal Spiritual Love has no boundary or perspective of any human being.

"If I speak in the tongues of men or of angels,
but do not have love,
I am only a resounding gong or a clanging cymbal.
If I have the gift of prophecy and can
fathom all mysteries and all knowledge,
and if I have a faith that can move mountains,
but do not have love,
I am nothing. If I give all I possess to the poor and
give over my body to hardship that I may boast,
but do not have love, I gain nothing.
Love is patient, love is kind. It does not envy,
it does not boast, it is not proud. It does not
dishonor others, it is not self-seeking,
it is not easily angered, it keeps no record of wrongs.
It always protects, always trusts, always hopes,
always perseveres."

1 Corinthians 13:1-5, 7

Heart to Heart 2

"I choose to love you in silence…
For in silence I find no rejection,
I choose to love you in loneliness…
For in loneliness no one owns you but me,
I choose to adore you from a distance…
For distance will shield me from pain,
I choose to kiss you in the wind…
For the wind is gentler than my lips,
I choose to hold you in my dreams…
For in my dreams, you have no end."
"I am so close, I may look distant.
So completely mixed with you,
I may look separate.
So out in the open, I appear hidden.
So, silent, because I am constantly talking with you."

Rumi

Part 3
The Healing

Pene Enochs

"Laugh when you can, apologize when you should,
and let go of what you can't change.
Life's too short to be anything but happy."

UNKNOWN

Five

> "Out of suffering have emerged
> the strongest souls; the most massive characters
> are seared with scars."
>
> Kahlil Gibran

LOSS AND HEALING

Where do I start with loss? Love and loss are certainly antagonistic, and yet there is a paradoxical synergy. It seems the duality of these two spheres are in the very makeup of our earthly reality. We have both in our lives, love and loss. There is no side tracking one nor the other. Love is the ultimate of one's goal in life, to love and be loved; yet there is a loss in all things. With to our final breath, sadness is evoked to someone, emanating some type of loss and pain.

Having loved without boundaries; one would assume there would be no loss. Just as there are many facets of love; we find loss brings about different types of emotional distress.

We think of loss as in a loved one, a relationship, or perhaps a circumstance. Having a loss in any area can be colored with varying shades of light and dark emotions. On the lower end of the scale, one may overcome loss quicker, simply because it is of minor importance. Interactions with higher emphasis, may demand deeper more intrinsic responses.

PAIN

Just thinking about loss, itself of a loved one or a relationship; may bring about unimaginable, and distressing emotional pain. Even in some instances the pain goes inward, affecting us physically, as well mentally. Saying our goodbyes seem to be the hardest thing to do. To let go of memories and emotions that were a part of you. The pain of letting go feels as though your heart is being torn apart, a part of your heart is missing. Asking yourself, "How can one go on with half a heart?" "How can one take another step, make another breath, or feel love again?" Countless physical tendencies come into play.

TEARS

Tears this lachrymal aspect, what do they serve? Some may say it cleanses the soul. Perhaps these sobs, sighs, and tears must be experienced before our healing process can begin. Nevertheless, latent memories still invading the mind, are an integral part in bringing about the ongoing flow of tears. So, what of this loss? Can one truly ever be whole and complete again?

What happens when we have a close relationship with a person, whether it be a family member, lover or friend; one minute a bonding relationship and in the next inconceivable moment they're gone. It leaves an empty chasm within oneself. With any loss comes aloneness, that perceptual separation. The word itself implies to be apart to separate, not together, but simply becoming a solitary entity. The severance of a loved one due to a death, in a relationship or merely backing away from a circumstance, can produce overwhelming, painful emotions. Being this solitary unit brings within oneself a manifestation of feelings pertinent to self. Unknowing of what was in the hearts of the other persons, we can only arrive at our own instinctual perceptions.

"The fear of death follows from the fear of life.
A man who lives fully
is prepared to die at any time."

MARK TWAIN

HEALING
Healing. What does this imply? There are so many aspects of healing. Knowing that the physical body can be healed through medicinal therapies; and yet there comes a deeper healing from within. Understanding, and trying to control our emotions; appear to be a bigger component of healing.

As in any viable earthly creation, there comes a time of cessation. A dissolution of our earthly exterior is finally eradicated, along with our illnesses, pains and fears. We are born, and we die, within our cycle of life. It is as though every creature on this earth has been allotted a certain number of heartbeats. We came into this world with nothing, and we leave this earth with nothing, but love and hopefully memories.

When trying to heal the heart, after losing discernible ideas or circumstances, this may in fact, bring about elements of tremendous emotional distress. After a lifetime of impassioned ups and downs, and therefore, continuing these elements of lifestyle; there comes a time of recognition, and the beginning of healing. Most likely by now, we should have realized that everything has a season. We see this in nature, even in beauty of the flower and butterfly. Everything on this planet has been given a time factor, a beginning and end. There is a time for grieving, of some loss in our lives; but as in the seasons, a change arrives, and then healing can begin.

While pondering the elements of loss, it brings us to a full circle. That implies our loss is merely the start of new beginnings. In due time, we find ourselves in the healing processes.

A TIME TO REBUILD
We can use every loss, as a lesson and experience. Every incident in our lives has purpose; depending upon how we

perceive and react to it. We have the choice! It may be easier to go down the slippery slope into self-pity, but there is a better way. The challenge is to find the solution. Many times, we must go deep within ourselves, and discover the meaning of our feelings and pain. Finding the answer, can bring about changes that can transform our inner self.

EMBRACE AND RELEASE

With every experience in our lives that is meaningful, we continue to have some recounting memories. In this moment, the embracing factor is important. Embracing every moment, every emotion is worthwhile; for this is what life is made of, emotions. At the time of disconnection, death or any other loss; we must turn our thoughts and feelings inward. Then we must release these earthly emotions into the outer most part of our world. Therefore, we can begin our new journey of healing. Realizing there are no quick fixes or magic pills to instantly change our feelings and emotions. Healing may appear to come in stages. Surrendering, embracing and releasing, is the beginning for our healing.

Pene Enochs

"What we have once enjoyed we can never lose. All that we love deeply becomes a part of us."

HELEN KELLER

Six

> "There is a time for everything,
> and a season for
> every activity under the heavens."
>
> ECCLESIASTES 1:1

THE ILLNESS

Recounting my life, I'm amazed that I have lived this long. With countless miscarriages and having over 20 surgeries, I am truly amazed at the resiliency of this earthly body. I'm truly astonished, that I continue to survive with these maladies. Not only with my earthly body in need of healing but my heart, mind, and sprit continue to be under construction of one stage or the other. Healing spiritually as well as physically, the body seems to have its own increments of space and time. Yet once again, we are not in control of this seemingly elemental development of healing. Unknowingly, we continue to strive forward in hopes of closure, a solution or perhaps a lesson brought forth. Being in a positive state of mind can bring about a rebirth to one's spirit. I believe this to be an important ingredient in healing. As to my healing experiences, *RE-BIRTH*, seems to be the component most closely aligned with me.

The Healing Within

As our lives are continually transforming, we can look back in amazement and see awesome miracles that have happened within our own bodies. Nonetheless, traveling in this unknown reality, once again there is that inevitable dualism of the human species. While dwelling betwixt a carbon based third dimensional human body, I have a sudden realization. That our subconscious/soul is even a bigger factor, when finding ourselves in these declining years.

From that first moment of birthing, begins the aging processes. Like all living species on this planet, the mere viability of our existence is within a brief span of allotted time. Living in health is the optimum in anyone's given perception of life. However, a change can happen instantaneously without notice. These earthly shells can exhibit disease of many variations. Causation of one's ill health or demise may be blamed on genetics, one's lifestyle, or even our spoken thoughts. Genetics and DNA, is the main factor in the genetic coding of one's existence. Traits as well as maladies are embedded within our body's DNA. Some of us are blessed with strong healthy bodies. There are those, who may be endowed with Mama's healthy heart, or perhaps Daddy's wonderful gift of music. Many of us have received unhealthy genes; as in my case, an unhealthy digestive system (from Grandma), kidney disorder (Grandpa), and visual problems (Father). Many of us start our life-cycle with these genes of disease from our very conception.

It seems we have started out in this body with templates from past tribal generations. Our lives as babes have been formed and molded into these impressions of humanness to live out our allotted time span. However, due to the power we give our thoughts, we have embedded within our own minds influences by our family, friends, and medias. What we do with our minds, is a choice we make. God gave us this marvelous brain, unfortunately we use only 10%. We may not realize that we our creators of our own world. We can be healthy, happy, joyful, or be unhappy, miserable, and negative by our thoughts and spoken words. We have choices as we mature, but it appears our genetic encoding is a comparable factor. As for me, the propensity for eye disorders, kidney problems and gastrointestinal problems are in my real world. For myself, believing that I have most likely received these maladies of life, from my genetics, lifestyle and my own thoughts. Thus, unknowingly becomes a precursor to a life of illness.

Lifestyles

As our bodies progress into later years the hindsight factor comes into play. "If I had known that I was going to live this long, I would've taken better care of myself." Introspectively, having this epiphany does not seem to deter our evolutionary path, nonetheless.

When in our Youth, we think we are invincible. Living in the moment, consuming whatever and burning our candle at both ends, so to speak, and perhaps consciously/subconsciously doing many things that are detrimental to our bodies and spirits. Rationalizing, that we are just like all the rest of "the *Gang*, "and just doing our "*thang*." Self-gratification seems to play a major role here. Whatever makes us feel good at the moment; and going along with the crowd, seems to be the journey many are taking.

Spoken Thoughts

It has been proven that like attracts like. Negative energies attracting other negative forces; whereas, positive energies attracting positive applications.

It isn't any wonder that our lives/world are affected by these quantum tendencies. We seem to sabotage ourselves, not only in the words that we speak; but also by our mental processes. As mere humans, our minds have taken on molding and patterning from the earliest years. Imposed upon our impressionable minds, are values, morals and beliefs, of this ménage of kith and kin. As toddlers we are told daily, "don't touch that, don't eat that, don't act like that." When we arrive into adulthood, it appears we have been inundated with ubiquitous negative as well positive contentions. It is no wonder that some of us are having problems living in this "*real*" world.

Knowing the brain is an exceptional organ, and without absolute answers to the makeup of its intuitiveness. We feed our subconscious continually. We do not seem to be conscious of the fact that our subconscious mind does not judge the positive or the negative that has been ingested.

Multiple books have been written about the brain. Having no expertise except for my own experiences, I have realized that my subconscious thoughts have led me into different unhealthy areas in my life. There were times I felt unworthy, unloved, rejected and insignificant; when in fact, these were lies. We tell ourselves these negative affirmations daily, and so our subconscious mind believes it. We feed into our subconscious minds from our very mouth. "I'm sick," "I can't do that," "no one likes me," "I'm unattractive." It is no wonder that we live in a world of chaos and continual illness. Therefore, we become the creators of our reality!

MY STORY

This leads me into my story, of healing. Many of my friends have encouraged me to write about my miraculous healing of

Crohn's disease. My story is about one person wanting to live; and what I did, may not have the same effect for someone else. This is simply my story and what measures I took to heal myself, with GOD'S direction.

"March on. Do not Tarry.
To go forward is to move toward perfection.
March on, and fear not the thorns or
the sharp stones on life's path.
Hitch your wagon to a star."

RALPH WALDO EMERSON

Seven

"Health is the greatest possession.
Contentment is the greatest treasure.
Confidence is the greatest friend.
Non-being is the greatest joy."

Lao Tzu

My Memory

The story of one my healing began when I was 44 years old. Being a neonatal nurse, a college student and a relatively new mother of adopted 2 year old, identical, twin girls; my life had become hectic, busy and stressful. My history of illness started in my childhood. Now, my illness had taken me downward into a spiral of infirmity.

Memory, has taken me back to a time of my first miraculous healing when I was only 21. In my previous draft, I omitted this part of my life however, I believe it has some significance in relaying the complete story of my healing.

Being pregnant with a 4 1/2-month-old fetus; and suffering from some unknown malady, my young body was in intense pain and desperation. After two weeks, my condition worsened, and there was no diagnosis at this time. Finally, one unforgettable afternoon; my condition worsens to the point of desperation. The rejection of my bowel content, was released through my projectile vomiting. In that moment, I was rushed into surgery and awaited the surgeon. The news had been relayed to my family; that to save my life they needed to perform exploratory surgery. It seemed I had a blocked bowel, that had become gangrenous. Most likely this occurred from the previous weeks of my undiagnosed condition. Now, my life was suspended in a delicate balance. The days that followed were precarious and uncertain.

On the second day, it appeared that the fetus I was carrying was no longer viable. My *precious Daddy* was with me almost every minute in these unbearable times. My Doctor had taken a break from this vigil. However, my Daddy remained and continued to hold my hand and comfort me. In the appointed time, my unborn fetus was expelled. I'm forever thankful for that unknown physician walking down the hall in my moment of need. After a month of confinement in the hospital, I was released, and the beginning of my long life of gut problems was created.

While encountering this proximity of death at 21, I was given a diagnosis of peritonitis, due to a blocked, gangrenous bowel. An interesting fact, that even to this day, the odds of surviving peritonitis is still a 50% chance.

CROHN'S DISEASE

It appeared Crohn's disease was to be my lifelong companion. After many bouts of illness and numerous surgeries, it appears my life on this earth had come to an end.

Many years of illnesses, surgeries and eight pregnancies; it was as though my body was telling me, enough is enough. It's evident that the ravages of Crohn's disease had placed me in a hopeless situation. Even though thinking that I was living life as usual, there was always the pain and symptoms of Crohn disease, which I simply dismissed. Unfortunately for me, my disease had progressed to the point of no return.

While working in surgery, my gastric surgeon had become one of my close friends. Upon realizing that I was very ill, and consulting with him, he immediately placed me in the hospital. After numerous tests, it revealed that my disease had ravaged my intestines, stomach and colon. My prognosis was dire. My friend had to inform me that I did not have long to live. He prescribed numerous medications, hoping to prolong my life for a few months.

After the head nurse had been given report on all her patients, she came into my room. She walked across the room, and sat on a chair next to my bed; expressing her sympathies for my dilemma. Knowing the story behind our adopted twins. She explained to me that she could not have children; and wondered if I would give her my twins, since I had very little chance of surviving another year. It seemed my little girl's lives were at a crossroad.

SHOCK SETS IN

Words cannot begin to tell you of the thoughts that were exploding within my mind. The fact that I didn't have long to live, my family and now these precious little girl's lives were at a crossroads. As usual, my mind always tries to analyze every little aspect of my life, even to the point of exhaustion. Considering that my darling little girls would be taken care of was something that I seriously contemplated. However, my other option was to take each day as it came; and so, my story continues.

I was looking back at the other chapter, that I had written on love and loss; and now I realized this was my real world. There was the real probability that my life would be over within a year. Where do you start, when given such earth-shattering news?

Believing there are no coincidences or accidents that have not been pre-orchestrated by Our Creator. Nonetheless, I began to question...OK God, what now? It seems in my mind I'm always questioning. There upon, my fragmented mind yet again, begins to work through it's labyrinth of circumstances. Sadness, pity, depression, fear and all other negative aspects of my situation were brought to the forefront. Having to deal with all this negativity and the awareness of leaving my family has left me devastated. My mind seemed to always be looking for answers, and here I was once more, my brain in continual motion.

A New Day

Going about my daily life was certainly challenging. While working only a couple of days a week; and caring for my family was taking a toll on my body. My husband Billy, knowing my Crohn's disease was advancing; encouraged me to take an acupressure class at the college. Having to expend energy outside my current responsibilities, was a hard choice to make. Nevertheless, starting my new classes, began my road to recovery. It was miraculous how the very touch of these acupressure points affected my body. Not only did I feel better, but my energy level was up. It was amazing!

One of my fellow classmates, Claudia, made an instrumental influence on me. While attending an herb class, it seemed Claudia knew more about herbs than our instructor. As a teenager, she had studied in the jungles of Mexico and acquired a wealth of information pertaining to medicinal herbs. Telling her of my dilemma, I hoped to glean knowledge from her expertise of herbs; and hoped to promote my healing. Claudia informed me of certain herbal compounds that

I should be taking and suggested that I visit a certain co-op herbal market, for more information.

Cowtown Co-Op

Cowtown Co-op, the herb store, is where my herbal education began. When I walked into the building, the sound of the bell on the door bell tinkled. Heralding the presence of someone new entering the store. I'm greeted by a gentleman, whose countenance had the appearance of a seasoned nature. The makeup of the store consisted of three rooms: when one walked into the first room, there was the overpowering smell of herbal properties. Also, an offering of home grown organic foods of one kind or the another had been displayed. On the counter resided an ancient cash register, a calculator and many brochures of health. The shelves on the wall contained various vitamins and supplements; along with other Instruments of alchemy.

Going into the interim section of the shop, I was overwhelmed by shelves of vats containing loose herbs. I was in awe and amazed at the different variety of herbs in medicinal potions offered. There were many herbs in glass containers, labeled and alphabetical order; just waiting to be served up for healing.

When I entered a small reading room, I took careful mental inventory of the offerings. My eyes were drawn to a small podium with a large reference book pertaining to herbs.

I assumed that anyone could, at a touch, open this incredible book of nature's healing properties. There were shelves of journals and books pertaining to herbs and healing; open to a novice like me. As I glanced around the room, on the wall there was a recipe for Jason Winters Tea. The Shopkeeper told me the Jason Winter's story. The story goes, that Dr. Winters had cancer; and traveled the world for remedies. He found no herb that could cure his disease. However, in the last stages of cancer he mixed three herbs together making a tea. He drank this combination of herbs, and his cancer was brought into remission. Now on the wall of this obscure little herb shop in Texas, there appeared to be a miraculous curative recipe.

During time spent in the co-op market, the most valued information was from the gentleman that opened the door to my knowing more about the healing properties of herbs. With his help, ascertaining which herbs would be beneficial, and with Claudia's influence, my journey to health began. A little note here, pill making took me to another level of patience, it was a laborious task filling my little gel capsules with herbs.

ROAD TO RECOVERY

Acupressure and herbs was the beginning of the road to my recovery. Diet became a big factor in my healing process about the time I began my regimen of herbs. As someone with digestive problems, the norm would've been to eat soft, bland foods, thereby eliminating any roughage or any foodstuffs hard to digest. On the contrary, for the next year my diet contained high fiber foods; mainly of vegetables and fruits, along with nuts (almonds). Also, I began to eat raw, whole grain wheat resembling raw oatmeal. My new lifestyle had begun. With the intake of herbs and drinking Jason Winters tea three times a day, the introduction of my new diet had been implemented.

Most likely, the most important factor in healing my Crohn's disease was through my own thoughts. My memory fails me to why or where I came to know about subliminal affirmations. Believing in divine intervention, I must take a stand on this, believing that God had led me in this direction, and was continuing to guide me. There were three cassette tapes that I listen to every minute of the day and night. This may be hard to believe, but it is nonetheless true.

A NEW VOCATION
Not only was my body changed, but so was a new vocation, for the remainder of my life. As long as I can remember, it seems I have always given back rubs; even while working in surgery. Having *"that touch,"* I was a requested circulating room nurse. During minor surgeries Dr. G sat on his stool, while I massaged his arthritic back. it was an ongoing joke, in surgery about Penny having a massage parlor. Twelve years

later that became a reality for me. When given the chance to pursue my massage therapist career, and having met all the requirements; it seemed logical choice for me. Knowing, from my own experience that massage and touch had a healing factor. Massage therapy opened yet another new world for me. There are so many wonderful stories to be told about my experiences, but I'll leave those stories for a later book. However, I need to preface this new career; simply because of the cassettes that I listen to in my massage therapy practice.

SUBLIMINAL CASSETTE TAPES

Getting back to my original thought about my tapes and listening to these subliminal affirmations. It seemed that I was plugged into continual affirmations at work, in my car, and at night while sleeping. For me the most important tape was the one of spiritual healing. For the mere fact of forgiveness and connecting with God was an essential element that my spirit needed most. My staying young tape seem to give me a new perspective about my body and mind. Subliminal affirmations about remaining young at heart and in mind, certainly came into play in the later chapters of my life. Finally, the recording about relieving pain; was crucial for living in this world of Crohn's disease.

Continuing this lifestyle for a year, and still taking medication every day; I had finally arrived at my *Waterloo*. This may seem gross or indelicate for most ears and eyes;

but it must be explained. Anyone with Crohn's disease, and dumping syndrome, can relate to the following. There is a constant elimination of one's bowel content, especially after a meal. So, it was not unlike my regular routine, except this day was to change the rest of my life with Crohn's disease. After the evacuation of my bowel, I knew something was different. Looking in the commode it was filled with a long snake like appearance, that of a shredded snakeskin after hibernation. Oh, the thoughts in my head.... thinking what have I done to myself? Who's going to take care of my family? Should I call my doctor? What? No, I didn't call my doctor, I simply waited. Fortunately for me my wait was successful. For I had no more pain, cramping and constant diarrhea. However, I need to clarify about the dumping syndrome. In my case, the multiple bowel resections (removal of 5 feet of intestines) earlier in my life had left me with this condition. Although, there have been natural ways to keep this in check.

After this timely bathroom episode, life became easier and better. My life had begun anew! No longer having the symptoms that I had been treated for, all my medications were discarded.

DISCLAIMER

I need to make a disclaimer here, if you are under a physician's care, please do not disregard their opinions. What worked for me, may not work for you. Although, with God's intervention and positive thoughts, I believe anything is possible!

Believing that everything had worked together in my case. Acupressure, herbs, diet, and positive thoughts were the keys to my success. Even though believing I had been healed, I still had a propensity for a kinked bowel. Having several episodes of a blocked bowel, whereupon calling my doctor, and he would admit me into the hospital. After self-acupressure manipulation and followed up by x-ray; the verification of no longer having a blocked bowel, and no signs of Crohn's disease was evident. They found no signs of Crohn's disease in my digestive system at all. One might say this is remission, you can call it anything you'd like; but it's been 34 years. Still in remission or healed, I'm leaving that up to you to decide for yourself.

Learning to live with one's disabilities, whether physical or mental is just another challenging aspect of life. We are here to live to our fullest, and to embrace all, as lessons in our reality.

"One word, frees us all of the
weight and pain in life.
That word is love."

SOPHOCLES

Part 4
On A Lighter Side

Pene Enochs

"And we should consider every day lost on which
we have not danced at least once.
And we should call every truth false which
was not accompanied by at least one laugh."

Friedrich Nietzsche

Eight

> "Don't be too timid and squeamish about your actions. All life is an experiment. The more experiments you make the better."
>
> Ralph Waldo Emerson

SINGLE AND A SENIOR CITIZEN

Here I am, SINGLE AND a SENIOR CITIZEN! What a wakeup call, to say the least!

Single, the definition of: being singular, isolated, separate, simple and sole, are among the varied descriptions now encompassing my new world. As far as defining senior citizen, this term showed up in my life around the age of 45. Offers from AARP arrived monthly. Becoming a senior citizen was quite different than what I expected at 45. It certainly was a game changer. You live your life unaware of the uncertainties of the future. Then you wake one morning, stare into the mirror and wonder, who the heck is this person? There are all the recognizable characteristics, but here is a face with aging skin and graying hair. I don't remember when this happened! There are lots of other things missing from my memory bank, which I won't mention at this time. This appears to be a contradiction to me. How can my face be so different from what my brain thinks, is this a joke? My brain seems to be stuck on my youthful idiosyncrasies, whereas this visual element of maturity is saying, "*hey, wait a minute!*"

OMG! Having arrived at this new serendipitous circumstance, leaves me a little befuddled and bewildered. Hey! That sounds like a song. I wonder if anyone has ever written a book on how to be a senior citizen?

YIKES! Now that I have arrived at this stage of decrepitude, my gray matter is impaled by descriptions of old age; such as, the elderly, golden-ager or geriatric generation, etc, etc, and so on. Is there no end to these unflattering descriptions of someone in my station of life? Being one or all the above, I would like to recommend perhaps to Mr. Funk and Mr. Wagnall a small modification regarding those of us of a more mature nature. Perhaps one tiny little change to the word *elderly*, could be a big start. Derivatives of the word implies old, tired, ancient, over the hill; and on your last leg, etc.

In my estimation, I have found that almost any age can be described as one or more of those listed.

Kason

One example might be my grandson Kason, who is 8 years old. With his day full of activities and finally home from school, we find the little man in deep concentration on his tablet. Of course, there are those times of changing from Tablet to Play Station or perhaps an evening of TV. Now back to an adjective to describe my grandson; the word tired is relative. For we know without a doubt, with all this exertion of brain power, such a one could certainly become tired and listless. Much too tired to pick up strewn clothing, his backpack or mislaid toys; and heaven forbid, an uncanny heaviness to his toothbrush. Kason, being one little example, and we know there are other younger people with the tired characteristic; even in my own family. I rest my case, on the definition of tired; as being one of those labels attached to us of a more seasoned nature.

Mr. Funk and Mr. Wagnall

Back to Mr. Funk and. Mr. Wagnall. May I be the first to suggest some new alternatives about describing us. As to being called "OLD," maybe we could be referred to as extraordinary, contemporary, ageless, or even specialized might be a better description.

"*Tired,*" now we've discussed this earlier, and we know this pertains to a lot of people. However, in referring to me, if you would please describe me as an extraordinary, ageless lady of minified energy, that sounds so much lovelier than a tired *old Lady*.

In reference to the ancient, over the hill and on your last leg scenarios; these also can pertain to a much younger generation. Point in case, back in the day, as a married teenager, and having a mother-in-law of a ripe old age of 39, I found this to be true. In my young eyes, everyone over 30 seemed "ancient" and pretty much "over the hill." Seeing my new mother-in-law at the age of 39, puts her in this category. It appeared her sedentary lifestyle had aged her brain as well as her body. In my young mind, my dear mother-in-law had become an over the hill, senior citizen at very early age. So, you see, the term over the hill is not limited to the senior citizen community. It can also apply to those of the younger generation.

JUST ME

Please let me emphasize right here, there are many more wonderful words to describe me other than ancient, over the hill and on my last leg. Some considerations might be that of stately, grand and respected. Personally, I find these to be much kinder than described as that One being over the hill; or that incredulous, on my last leg.

If you haven't already guessed by now, being single and a senior citizen means different things to different folks. As for me, I do not attach a label to myself nor my friends. Besides, it seems our minds do not age at the same pace as our chronological body. For some of us in my group, our thoughts are so much younger that our earthly bodies. We have been labeled as childish, and told that it appears that we never grew up. Alas, someone has to do it; so, I guess that makes me leader of the pack. Yes, we sometimes forget, and we have been known to do foolish, childish things…. So, if you ever happen to see an *extraordinary*, *stately* and *grand*, red headed lady, riding on the back of a motorcycle…. Look closely! It might just be *me*.

Pene Enochs

"Don't walk behind me; I may not lead.
Don't walk in front of me; I may not follow.
Just walk beside me and be my friend."

ALBERT CAMUS

Nine

> Since you cannot do good to all,
> you are to pay special attention to those who,
> by the accidents of time,
> or place, or circumstances,
> are brought into closer connection with you.
>
> Saint Augustine

HEARTS TOUCHING

It is truly unbelievable how interactions of total strangers can enmesh and mingle within our very presence. Astounding as it may seem, one might wonder why this has not happen before, in this point of time, or has it? Seemly, the stages around our lives are culminated within our daily existence. However, goals and responsibilities seems to warrant most of our time. Having interactions with first loves, friends, and family are the most important at the time. When meeting someone that touches your life in an extraordinary and familiar way, is mind blowing. When we meet that special one making that instinctual union, a familiar bond is formed; it is truly a phenomenal interaction. The exchange between two individuals in this flow of energy can produce an exciting connection.

Another Year

A new year has brought me, again, experiencing, and connecting with various new people. As always, I am honored and blessed with touching heart to heart with so many wonderful individuals. I continue to be overwhelmed, when these special "Ones" come into my life, and we make an instant connection. Prone to analyzing my life situations to the max, leaves me also analyzing my present position.

In the recesses of my mind and wondering why my life has been touching these diverse individuals; I answer, my own question. Knowing that everything has purpose and meaning. I realize this miraculous meeting can be helpful in experiencing spiritual motivations. There can also be exhortations from a lesson, to be acquired.

Last year and realizing a few of my heart felt connections were merely for a transient moment, no matter how compelling. These lessons experienced were invaluable. They made new interactions more enlightening, and on a more soul to soul contact. Which brings about in my life, a certain kind of permanence, an acceptability of sorts.

TOM

Starting with the present time, but going back 45 years when talking about Tom. My first meeting with Tom was at the baseball park. Tom and my husband were coaches for a little league baseball team. We were friends with Tom and Peggy when our boys were young. Over the years with our families growing up and moving into different directions, our contact was sporadic. Even though, living in a small town, I've not interacted with Tom for many years. It was surprising when I saw him at one of the dances. It seems his wife Peggy passed away three months after my Billy. Being in the same club, that being widow/widowers we had a mutual bond. There were moments of loneliness, being out of touch and simply not knowing what to do with ourselves. Dancing was in our blood, it seemed a good way to get out of the house, and be around other people in similar circumstances.

It seemed we just gravitated to one another. Most likely because of the simple fact that we had known one another for such a long time. It made that sister/brother relationship come out.

If someone were to have told me a couple of years ago, that I would be out almost every night with Tom, I wouldn't have thought it possible. Nevertheless, here we are. Since driving isn't one of my favorite things to do, especially at night, Tom has become my wheels. So, where Tom goes, therefore I go. (most of the time)

Speaking of dancing, there's a subject that needs a little more explanation. Our circuit dance establishments are many and varied. From parties and dances with our widow/widower's group to traveling many miles just to try out a new band. The Craig Street dance was my first introduction to the group. The name of this club is called the Half-Century Club. Keep in mind that our club, the half-century club has very few members that are in their 50's. This group Is composed of persons closer to the century mark rather than the half-century. Just because there may be snow on the rooftops of many of these folks, it does not constrain them from jitterbugging, waltzing or twisting to music of the 50s. Keeping in mind that these seniors range from age 55 to 100 It is so amazing to me, seeing the energy level and vitality of life in each person. The energy expended within this group could rival someone in their 40s It is incredible to see everyone dancing, laughing and enjoying the moment.

BERNICE

I would like to start from that very first moment that Bernice, my friend, played a big role in the early days of my widowhood. Having lost her husband a few years earlier, made her aware of how climatic my world was about to become. She was instrumental in getting me out of the house and into this new world of being a widow, single and alone. It is through her insistence; my dancing routine began. If it had not been for Bernice, I may to this day be sitting at home.... knitting. However, that wasn't to be, (Besides, I hate knitting.) Again, I am so thrilled to have a caring friend like Bernice.

Ray

Bernice had introduced me to her neighbor Ray at one of the dances. We seem to hit it right off and we became instant friends. Ray was an excellent dancer, we had tremendous fun going to the dance clubs. Even though Ray was over 6 feet tall, he was quite agile and smooth on his feet, as we waltzed across the floor. To this day when I hear the band play Waltz Across Texas, I cannot help but think of Ray.

One night as I was working myself around the room, greeting everyone. I was always keeping an eye out for a pretty new dance partner for Ray. After my butterfly reception, I return to my chair next to Ray. When I sat down, Ray turned to me and said, "I found me a girl!" Whereas, I excitedly remarked, "Well, that is wonderful Ray." He replied, "Yes, I saw her back across the room, when she turned around.... then he placed his hand on my arm....it was YOU!" Even though I knew that I was not the right girl for Ray, I was very honored to think that he would even choose me.

Ray was the gentle giant, sweet and funny. He was the first man that entered my life, after the passing of my husband. I was honored to call Ray my friend.

First Date

Ray was my first date after many years! Keep in mind, here I was, a "widow," "single" and very "mature." I remember well that evening, of my first dinner date. I felt almost like a teenager, not knowing exactly what was about to happen. It seemed Ray had not had a date for quite a while also. So, we were both, somewhat apprehensive. As we entered the dining room, it was evident that the ambience was that of an Italian flair, quiet and cozy. While sitting at our intimate little table, we seem to have troubled conversing, there were long lapses of silence. Somewhere in between the salad and the entrée, Ray got a phone call. It seemed his daughter Jessica was wondering how the date was going. Well, the date went just as though two teenagers had gotten together for the first time.... weird, strange, and awkward.

I must make another little post script, my dates with Ray improved drastically. The next dates were wonderful. Ray was the man I had come to know, charming, sweet, kind and funny. We had many days of dancing and simply having fun. Even though our lives seldom touch anymore, my fond memories remain intact. Ray was certainty a "Godsend" when I needed a "*friend*" the most.

"Without friends, no one
would choose to live,
though he had all other goods."

ARISTOTLE

Ten

"A good life is when you assume nothing,
do more, need less, smile often,
dream big, laugh a lot, and
realize how blessed you are."

Unknown

ENTERING THE BALLROOM

As I walk into the ballroom, I noticed many attractive and lovely people. Everyone seem to open their arms to me, and I to them. There is a surprising number of couples in relationships of one kind or the other, while the remainder of us are single. All are accepting and friendly, and my first encounter was with a lady named Sheila, "Doll." (my name for her, because she reminded me of a beautiful little doll).

Sheila "Doll"

Sheila's, alias "Doll", her demeanor was bubbly and full of life, as well her beautiful and sweet countenance. It is so special to me when arriving at a dance; and see her beaming, beautiful face. In her excitement, she always greets me with hugs and wonderful affirmations. Our exuberance in our meeting one another at every dance is evident to everyone in the room. Of course, it might have been due to our squeals, laughter and behavior, seemingly actions of a "*teenager*" instead of a mature "*Senior citizen*." Not only did we hit it right off, but we had so many common life experiences. OMG, how lucky am I to have made such an amazing friendship? My Sheila," Doll "was one of many people that composed my new life. Sheila has become my "*Soul Sister.*"

As I glide around the edge of the ballroom floor, I am greeted by familiar faces. There is Myrna, D.D., a committed couple from our widow/widowers group. George, is a single gentleman, who enables many single ladies a dance partner. Now, we come to Tom (Rosy); whereas, I need to make a short comment about Tom. Rosy, is "*Pecks Bad Boy.*" He is truly the little boy, that never grew up, being that he most likely pestered all the girls in the fourth grade. His reputation is still intact, for he is still aggravating the girls (mostly me), with no letup in sight. I believe Rosie and I are kindred spirits, however, in different ballparks!

"S<small>ISTERS</small>"
I called these two girls my "sisters," Frances, Irene and I made an instant connection. While Frances was the quieter and more retiring of my newly proclaimed sisters, it left Irene the

more rambunctious of the two. There was a surprised look on Rays face when I introduced Irene as my sister. A little *insignificant* note here, Irene is Chinese. With a surprised look on his face, he looked at her and then at me. Whereas, Irene quips, "We have different mothers, our father got around a lot." I also need to mention a known fact about Irene, there's never a dull moment when she's around. Irene is high energy, enthusiastic and fun to be around.

Many members were from the widow/Widowers group, and I feel right at home by their presence. The consensus being, most were from this group. Therefore, we were all out to have fun and to enjoy ourselves. We appeared like one big family. In actuality, we probably saw one another more, than we did with our immediate families.

ARLINGTON
When I entered the Arlington dance club I am welcomed by C.L. with open arms, and a welcoming hug. On the long table at the entrance, Roger is ready to make change and issue a raffle ticket to some unsuspecting lucky person. After passing the entrance table we encounter the welcoming line. Thelma, Carolyn, "Georgie," Fran and Norma are always the first in line just waiting to welcome everyone. This welcoming committee is there every week to greet us. Arlington is one of our favorite places to dance, so we go regularly, twice a week. Where else in town could you go to a dance

with a live band, fun loving people and a snack for six bucks? I rest my case!

EXUBERANT CONTACTS

Traveling in this new circle of dance clubs has brought so many special people into my life, and it seems without end. I'd like to expound upon a couple of folks that have recently entered my life/heart.

CECIL

Cecil is one of my "*comrades,*" when entering the dance arena, A little note about our dancing skills. When we dance, it is unlike no other couple. Our moves and steps are truly our own, perhaps, unrecognizable to those who have mastered the art of dance. We managed to twirl, spin and move to our own rhythm. So far, no one has questioned are ability to dance the waltz or the jitterbug.... whew! Of course, our job is to fulfill our mission, to having fun!

"DARLIN" AND "LIL BOBBY"

Darlene "Darlin" is another friend that I greet rather loudly. When I enter the room, sometimes I hear a loud commotion. Darlin' and Little Bobby (Robert) have spied me. We run to one another as though we have not seen one another for months, even though it has only been a day or two. This silver haired duo makes the most delightful couple. *"Darlin"* is one of those exquisite, ageless, and beautiful women. Of course, "*Lil Bobby*" is not so bad either.

I am beginning to think that I may have corrupted some of my friends by my exuberant personality. Because I am finding more and more of my friends acting just like me!

BUTTERFLY DANCE

Beginning my night of embracing each and every person in the room. I have been called a "*Butterfly*," I suppose, because it seems I flit from one person to the next. Of course, I take that as a complement! As I begin my butterfly dance, I interact with every lady and gentleman. Each lady Is adorned with her own unique style. Whether it be a manicured coiffured appearance, an elegant bejeweled attire; or dressed in western regalia; all are beautiful. As to the gentlemen attire, casual is the common appointment of dress. However, many are bedecked in beautiful western shirts of unusual patterns and design. Along with boots, belts, and cowboy hats; which puts them in a category equal to the ladies. Here again, I must make note, Lorenzo is one of these fantastic dressers. Truly, I am blown away, at his wardrobe of such unusual shirts. He is the fashion plate for all those dressing in western style. I must make a post script right here. Of course, in my estimation Lorenzo, is the forerunner in this area of fashion. But now I must conclude, that many men of our dancing group are wearing spectacular western shirts, and western attire. Point in case, Ronnie, Robert, and Phil are certainly among the best dressed in the male western attire category.

Suzy and Ed

There are so many beautifully dressed ladies and gentlemen in this group, I hardly know where else to go. So, I will go to my beautiful little Suzy and Ed. They are always dressed perfectly in their western attire. Suzy, is the epitome of being dressed the most appropriately for any night. Her wardrobe alone is astounding to me. Suzy's "*accouter*" is always perfect, from her head to her toe!

Now as for Ed, he is truly a tall drink of Texas Water! Always fitted in his Texas gear, from his cowboy hat right down to his cowboy boots. I need to add a description to his hat, he has placed his *winning* tickets in the hat band. Of course, when the time arrives, and prizes are to be awarded; he is the first one to the stage to claim his prize. Alas, being a little bit disappointed, it seems he has the right number…. but not on his ticket! It appears that it is the number of his apartment! In addition to the winning tickets, that haven't transpired, I need to add another little tidbit about Ed. He tries to celebrate his birthday on every occasion, and he even gets by with it sometime. Ed's funny demeanor and joking nature enlivens any room; and we are all entertained by his presence.

Another little note about Ed and Suzy, love has made its way into their lives. We know that Love is a powerful emotion, and it is certainly evident with Ed and Susie. When their dance begins, there is no one else in the room but them.

Eleven

"The philosopher soul dwells in his head,
the ports so are in his heart;
the singer so lingers the back his throat,
but the soul of the dancer abides in all her body"

Kahlil Gibran

DANCING AROUND THE CHAIR

Having need to explain further about these dances; but keeping in mind, the fact being, that primarily women live longer than men. Therefore, the ratio in the men's favor is around 12 to one. There is a lot to say in this matter. Many of the guys have attached themselves one way or the other to some of these lovely ladies. Now, this leaves a lot of us gals without dance partners. However, there are some couples that don't display that territorial division. So, it allows us to dance with their significant other. For one to visualize this dance, just place yourself in the majority category, that being, one of the 12 to 1 single ladies. Two chairs are placed at opposite corners. Now being with the majority, we line up behind the chairs. When finally, our time comes, we walk around the chair and wait our turn to dance with the next man. Whereas we now dance to the other corner, and the dance continues. This allows us to dance with many different partners. All of this is going on with an extended song, played by a favorite country/western band. A perfect time to interact with different gentlemen, and sometimes dancing with several new partners.

THE MONTANA BAND

My favorite band is The Montana Band. Band members Larry, Dayton, Buddie, Dick, and Dixie always manage to entertain us with their music and wonderful singing styles. Each member of the band has years of experience in the music industry. The harmonies are special among the band, and each have their individual sound.

A little note about Dixie, not only is she a drummer, but her voice is like *"butter"*. When she sings Lisa, everyone stops their dancing, and listens to her beautiful voice. *Needless to say, I am a member in her fan club.*

On my first encounter with the band, I became enamored with the harmonica player, Larry. I was smitten after hearing that "*first*" note. Not only does he play a mean harmonica, but he's also gifted with the guitar and has a terrific voice. I should say Dayton was a close second with his mellow vocal tones; it was as though he was singing just to me. It is no wonder I'm their number one "fan." Although, a cute little gal named Marie seems to have seniority over me. As of yet, I have never had a song dedicated to me, like Marie. Darn, all this time I thought Dayton was singing just to me!

Correction! After many weeks, I finally had a song dedicated just to me! Of course, I'm sure it had nothing to do with my whining, cajoling, and bemoaning.

CLARK

I do believe Clark is the most unforgettable person that I have met during the chair dance. (In fact, he is likely one of the most unforgettable character I have ever met in my life) Having never met him before; I was quite unprepared for his quick wit and humor. While dancing in the chair dance, I had to excused my dancing because of my shoes. My sandals were evidently not appropriate for dancing, for they were apparently sticking to the floor. Whereas, Clark stops dancing, looks down at my shoes, looking up at me and quips, "only Jesus wore those kinds of shoes!" This was my introduction to Clark. Later, after meeting Dot, his beautiful new wife of only a year; I was hit with another zinger. Teasing with him about how he happened to win this beautiful lady in marriage. It only took a few seconds for his comeback, I was pregnant." Only Clark could come up with that line. What a combination! Her beauty and his witty humor and candor. This group of folks would certainly be a little bland and dull without this couple's interaction. P.S. He is a great dancer, of course Dot most likely taught him!

Newlyweds

When speaking of Love, I would be remiss if I did not mention two of my favorite people, Barbara and Ralph. It so happened that I was there at the very beginning. Seeing this couple in love, made it seem as though life in these matured years, may have real promise. To be witness to these two-loving people has been exciting.

Barbara and Ralph

While standing behind the chair, my approaching dance partner was none other than Ralph, tall, gray haired, and with the most amazing smile. His happiness was evident, and a light seem to shine from within him. His face beaming, eyes that were shining and that wonderful toothy grin, was evident of his adoration for his beloved Barbara. This tall, willowy, graceful gal, was his perfect match. This couple fit together perfectly; and to this day, their dance has become one of effortlessness and grace. Love and happiness is indisputable, wherever they go.

OLIVER AND DOLLY
While on the subject of couples and dancing; I need to talk a little about Oliver and Dolly. Of the many excellent dancers in the group; in my estimation, these two are the most graceful and elegant dancers of all. Even after foot surgery, it did not keep Dolly off the dance floor for very long. She was back in the groove within a few weeks. Although, she was supporting a surgical boot upon her foot, it did not seem to deter their smoothness and exceptional dance style. Now among her dance trophies, she needs an award for her tenacity and perseverance.

I am in admiration, of the dance styles and proficiency of so many of these couples. As a senior citizen (there must be a nicer word), it is wonderful to be a part of this group of ladies and gentlemen, that have become a big part of my life. In this stage of life, yet again, I am blessed to have this opportunity to interact with such diversified and caring people.

"Impart as much as you can of
your spiritual being
to those who are on the road with you,
and accept as something precious
what comes back to you from them."

ALBERT SCHWEITZER

Twelve

> "To laugh often and much;
> to win the respect of intelligent people
> and the affection of children…
> to leave the world a better
> place….to know even one life has
> breathed easier because you have lived.
> This is to have succeeded."
>
> RALPH WALDO EMERSON

THE JOURNEY CONTINUE

As my journey continues, on this road of continual change, I shouldn't be surprised when one of these wonderful heart-to-heart connections are made. Unsuspecting, but always open and receptive to these gifts of the heart. My life experiences are filled with an occasional "heart to heart" extraordinary connection. While some have been brief, however, they are nonetheless compelling. So much so, that I am recounting their stories.

No matter how brief, when someone enters your life. The most important thing to remember, they were meant to be there. When a close interaction with an individual takes place, we gain in some way, whether it be in pain or ecstasy. The energy expended with others is relevant to our own energies. Therefore, the exchanging of the essence, of one to another can bring about a permanent interaction.

RENA

When arriving at the Burger Barn; I begin my butterfly dance. Talking with each and every one. As I approached Gladys, one of my favorite karaoke singers, sitting in a booth with four other ladies. She introduced me to each one. When introducing her sister Rena, I felt a real camaraderie, an Instant like. It seems I was having another miraculous heart to heart connection, with this special lady. This little gal was outgoing and exuberant; cute as a button, with a sassy pink bow in her hair. As we talked, she told me about her daughter in New York and about her successful dance studio. Rena told me that she had been taking *Swahili* dance lessons, at her daughter's studio.

Since I'm always interested in learning new dances, Rena was ready and willing to be my new dance instructor. When a certain musical rhythm began playing, she started showing me the movements and steps. The dance told a story of communication and life of the Swahili, particularly the women.

YES! I had learned a new dance, an African *Swahili* dance. How great was that!

New Friend

Going back to my chair in the back of the room, looking up toward the stage, I see a young man, looking at me and doing moves of this new dance. Standing up, I began to follow his movements. Eventually, I moved up to the stage where my new young friend was dancing, we finished our *Swahili* dance together. This young black man touched my heart; not only did we connect with Rena's *Swahili* dance; but even with his disability, he was able to connect with me! This was truly a double blessing for me. You just never know when you might entertain angels!

While talking with Rena, I felt as though I had known her forever. She talked about her life and how she and her three sisters has sung together all their life. When it came time sing, she and Gladys sang their song without the other sisters. Even so, it was a treat for all of us. We laughed, danced and had this memorable time together. We exchanged telephone numbers; and were excited to know when we would see one another again. In the following weeks, we were reunited at the widow/widowers meeting. Never missing a beat, we took up right where we had left off. We discussed a visit to Pennsylvania, when her sister Gladys, had planned a trip.

Curve in the Road
Unfortunately, there was a curve in the road. I did not make it to Pennsylvania to visit my new friend. On her return home, she became ill. Several months after our meeting, she succumbed to cancer. Even though our connection was one of short duration; concern and love grew out of this significant interaction. As for me, there is no doubt in my mind, that she is doing her Swahili dance in heavenly places.

R. L.
As I entered the ballroom, I was greeted by familiar faces. We have been on the dance circuit for several months now, but it was the first time to visit this new club. Although, many of the dancers here, are regulars at the other clubs. It seems there are always those new and interesting faces to encounter.

While the night unfolded, the infamous "chair" dance was introduced. All the ladies begin lining up behind the two chairs at opposite ends of the room. it is obvious that some of these couples have taken lessons; which was evident by their dance moves and style. so, it is always exciting to dance with one of these accomplished dancers.

Recognition
Standing behind the chair and waiting my turn, a stranger takes my hand. He is tall and thin, but muscular. His eyes appear dark, yet dancing with light. His perfect teeth are the

ultimate paradigm of a Crest toothpaste commercial. His elegant demeanor made him a perfect model for GQ magazine. With that first moment of contact, there is an immediate jolt of familiarity. Locked in one another gaze, without any words, a bond of recognition began to emerge.

It seems we cannot keep our eyes off each other. When he dances with others, my eyes continually searching the floor for a glimpse of him. When I'm dancing in the arms of another, I am aware of his dark eyes following me. As he dances by, he looks my way and gives me that resplendent smile. It seems evident with this surreal physical and spiritual gravitation to R, L., a familiar bonding has occurred.

FLEETING CONNECTIONS

It is interesting to note, there has been very little communication or contact with one another. Even so, the brief times of conversation, seem to lead to the fact of knowing a deep affection for one another. Conceivably, from a time of long past. With each brief encounter with R. L., we find ourselves in sympathetic agreement with the recognition of simply, the past. Of where, when or even why hasn't been revealed. There is a feeling of unspoken intimacy, or even on a higher level; perhaps that of a poignant love. For all one knows, there may be some unfinished circumstances that must be healed.

That Old Feeling

Every encounter with R. L. brings about an interesting physical response. It's a vibration, that I have experienced with others with whom I have made a deep connection. It has been said that we sometimes meet individuals of the same "frequency." For most of my life, even at a young age, I've somewhat had the ability to pick up on this phenomenon. It certainly isn't any wonder that I'm having this resonance with R. L., simply because I feel a closeness with his vibration. These recent reverberations seem to transpire with much more intensity and strength, much more than any other person. As a result, revealing different emotional and intrinsic reaction from one another. Believing this event is common with everyone. Thus, having the ability to pick up on another's emotional vibration. The physical idiosyncrasies of these vibrations can in some instances be felt as chill bumps, or goosebumps. Also, another way, is the sensation of feeling your hair standing on end. When both individuals align themselves with these vibrations, there is a synchronicity and intuition that prevails.

Whether we consciously believe it or not, all our life we interact with others, and it molds us into the person we become. Thus, it is so awesome to contact that one with which we find a close kinship. Each person that comes into our life, makes a difference. How we choose to interpret these experiences are left up to each one of us. An awareness with that special person, can produce helpful and loving interactions, or perhaps a life lesson to be learned, in the present time.

SOULMATE

The most amazing fact about meeting R. L. Is that he is my "*Soulmate.*" Not only have I encountered a brief interlude with my "*Twin Flame,*" now I have been touched by someone who fulfills all my innermost feelings. Finding R. L. In this world of billions of people has been another miracle. This encounter, even for such a brief moment, has brought me to recent memories. Once again, I am astonished. My mind is in a constant state of wonder and amazement at the meeting of such an exceptional person. This brief connection has been very exciting and an interesting chapter in the metamorphosing of my life.

OWEN

The first time I met Owen, who was only 4 years old. He was apparently taller than most children of his age. His hair was cropped short, resembling the color of wheat, and his eyes were bright with an inner sparkle. Owen, baby sister, and mama had been invited over for dinner that evening, by my "self-proclaimed son," Jessie.

I was sitting in the den, with Ipad on my lap, and doing my usual thing, writing. After introductions, there was a quick tour upstairs (mostly to scope out the toy room). Owen, returns to the den, walks over to where I'm sitting, and looking me right in the eye asks; "what are you doing?" I explained to him that I was writing. Whereas, he replies, "what are you writing?" My response was, "I'm writing a book. Without hesitation, he replies, "I'm going to write books too." Trying not to sound too condescending, I told him that was nice; and he can do anything that he put his mind to. Never giving this much thought, just assuming this little boy was simply responding to what I had said to him.

I would like to make a statement here. Never assume anything about anyone at any age. Because what followed.... astounded me.

4 YEAR OLD SAGE

Owen came into the kitchen; and walked over and stood near the oven, about two feet from where I was cooking. Whereas, he began an in-depth discussion about God and Jesus. The first statement out of his mouth was.... you know, "I'm God". Astonished at his direct statement; but I went along with his acknowledgment. Actually, this is no surprise to me, since I am God also. I explained to him, "Yes I knew that he was God, we were made by God and therefore, God is in all of us."

He began to tell me about Jesus; and about the people who killed him. We talked about Christ, and his purpose in coming to this place. He knew that Christ was the example for all of us.

KEEP IN MIND, THIS IS A FOUR YEAR OLD CHILD!
I was absolutely blown away. In all my life, I have never met such an intuitive, precocious child. Having a conversation with this young child was like talking to my minister. I began to wonder about his first years, perhaps some influence with his family and church. Maybe that could shed some light on my questions, about where he obtained his spiritual knowledge. However, on the contrary, Owen's mom is not a churchgoer. It is my understanding that she has no spiritual beliefs. Now, I am truly in a state of shock and disbelief.

My meeting Owen, has absolutely been one of the most outstanding, wonderful connections that I've ever had the pleasure to encounter. This is, one of my most unforgettable experiences. Even though, I have not seen Owen again, he will forever be in my memory, as well this book. His brief encounter into my life, was like the *breath of an angel...innocent and heavenly.*

For Frank and R.C

LAST DANCE

"There seems to be a perpetuity premise...
of love, loss, and healing.
We love, enjoy and treasure the moments
of these happy times.
All the while, knowing that our moments
on this earth are limited;
and likened unto our Infamous measured heartbeats.
When we lose that special person that has been
in our dancing life, there's always
thoughts of these exceptional ones.
It may have been their smile, a laugh
or maybe just the way they danced.
We store thoughts away in our memory.
To bring them forth, in a day of remembrance,
and bear us to mind,
of those who have left us far behind.
There's no time to be sad,
for knowing we too, are only a breath away
from our eternal dance.

Pene Enochs

I know not what tomorrow brings,
As for me, this may be my final dance.
So, think kindly of me and remember,
my smile…my laugh…or my funny dance."

Pene

And said unto him, "Hearest thou what these say?" Jesus saith unto them, "Yea; have ye never read, Out of the mouth of babes and sucklings thou hast perfected praise?"

MATTHEW 21:16 KJV

Thirteen

*"Keep your heart with all vigilance,
for from it flow the Springs of Life."*

Proverbs 4:23

PLAYING IT FORWARD

After the death of my husband, I found myself at a loss. Here I was with so much time on my hands and without any kind of direction. Being a caregiver for so many years had left an empty space within me now. I think these feelings must be akin to the "empty nest syndrome." Here I was, a healthy, energetic, mature lady without a purpose. So, on this Saturday, I chose to begin a new endeavor, that of visiting a nursing home near my church. A few weeks before Easter, we in the South, observe Mardi Gras. There are always parties and parades one can go to celebrate the event. After gathering countless Mardi Gras beads, I summoned my grandson Kason to help me on my new adventure.

One reason for choosing this nursing home was the fact that I knew someone that lived there. I remember Richard, who regularly attended my church had maneuvered his wheelchair up to the front of the sanctuary. Whereby, at the appointed time he began to sing his beautiful original song. His words were like a love song to God, all the while, allowing us the privilege of hearing his innermost prayer. It is apparent to me, even if we are impaired with some type disability, we can still use our talents. When using our gifts to our fullest capacity, it is to achieve some significance in our life. Even to the smallest of our recognized talents, it can bring about a blessing. As for myself, I believe the most wonderful aspect when using and giving of our gifts is the feelings we receive in return.

Mardi Gras Beads

While handing out our Mardi Gras beads, we were blessed with many smiles and appreciation for our tiny little gift. We were greeted with big smiles and some laughter; which touched my heart. For such a tiny little act of kindness, and to receive back so much in return was truly awesome. Being amid this myriad of patients ranging from middle age to the elderly, I find myself being very thankful and blessed. There but for the grace of God go I.

Several residents stand out in my mind. Some are confined to their beds and are unresponsive. It seems I am drawn to them. Some can communicate in some way while others are in their own world. I find myself touching and caressing those that seem to have need of a touch. As I put myself in their situation, I begin talking about how much they are loved not only by God, but also me. Hearing is the last of our senses that leave our body. Placing myself in this condition I speak the words that I would like to have spoken to me. Words of appreciation and thankfulness and being special and loved. I do not know if they can hear my words, however, I pray that they hear Gods.

GAIL AND MITZI

As I entered the room of this tiny little lady, I was greeted with a sweet smile and crippled little hands. Stroking her hands and face, I tell her who I am and ask her if she would like to have some beads. Not only is she impaired physically but also vocally. I am unable to understand what she is saying, yet I'm able to understand her in other ways. She made it known that she wanted the green beads and I told her those were my favorite also. As I looked into her little face, I told her that she was loved by me and it seemed to be reciprocated. We seem to go to a higher level of communication. Again, I have made a connection with this fragile little lady that has touched my heart.

Mitzi, another wonderful lady that I have encountered on this new journey is a beautiful black lady with a smile on her face that could light up any room! Even though she was confined to her bed, she had a countenance of being alive and in the moment. Another special person has touched my heart and it is a certainty that I will return and visit my new friends.

My Return

I'm thinking perhaps that I could certainly give my time once a month. However, I am drawn back within a week. The gift that I received from these precious ones in the nursing home far exceeded whatever I could ever give to them. So back I went for another visit. On this valentine weekend, I passed out heart-shaped balloons. As I entered Mitzi's room I presented her with a red heart balloon. She was thrilled to see me and I was excited to see her again. She continued to say such glorious things to me, calling me her angel. It was the most uplifting moment for me. I am overwhelmed at the acceptance I have been given.

Not recalling why, the subject of writing came up, she told me of her desire to write a book. In return, I mentioned to her of my little book that had just been published. She immediately asked me for a book; I told her that I would certainly bring her one.

On my next visit, I decided to take stuffed animals. On this afternoon, some of the residents were sitting on the porch and several others were in the lobby. When I walked in it seemed several recognize me. Some were sitting in chairs, wheelchairs and others were walking around in the area. The nurses station was in the middle of all the intersecting wings and seem to be the hub of most of the interaction. Everyone was friendly and smiling as I approached them with my little gifts again. I find it amazing how such a small thing such as a teddy bear can bring about so many smiles and laughter.

MY LITTLE BOOK

On a previous visit, I had given Mitzi one of my books. She explained she had finished it and had given one to her roommate to read. As I looked around the room her roommate was not there. When I questioned Mitzi about her friend, she replied, "she passed away this morning." She told me that her friend had read my book the night before. Well, I must say that was a bit of shocking information. To have someone read my thoughts before their demise was truly a humbling experience for me. We can never know our influence on someone, whether it be in a book or in a spoken word.

 My visits to the nursing home have continued. There's a continual change. Some have left this earthly place, while others have gone home, and of course there are those that remain. There are always new faces and new personalities emerging when a need arises for confinement. So, I take on this job, as a butterfly persona, and I flit one to the other looking for that heart to heart connection.

Heart to Heart 2

"Just as the wave cannot exist for itself,
but is ever a part of the heaving surface of the ocean,
so, must I never live my life for itself,
but always in the experience which is going on around me."

ALBERT SCHWEITZER

Part 5
My Persecutive

Pene Enochs

"Let love flow so that it cleanses the world.
Then man can live in peace,
instead of the state of turmoil he has created
through his past ways of life, with all material interests
and earthly ambitions."

Sai Baba

Fourteen

"Everything in the universe is within you.
Ask all from yourself."

Rumi

TRANSFORMATION

Looking back over our lives, we can hopefully realize and see the significance of love, loss and healing. No one is immune to these many dispositions of emotions. Emotions flow daily in our life, not unlike the ocean's tide, surging and ebbing.

Our physical existence began at birth with the stark reality of entering a world without perceived memory and physically helpless. We flow along in this life journey, where we are instinctively directed by our cognition and intuition. However, many disregard any spiritual guidance, in this direction, due to disbelief, unconcerned or merely oblivious to these higher realms of reality. Many have been directed and led from their earliest recollection by the misguidance of others.

YOUTH
Youth has a way of simply living day by day. Striving in a microcosm that revolves about themselves; living within a hectic world of relationships, workplace and self. Trying to cope with everyday situations, each with its complexing and overriding rituals.

Living in a world of illusion and consequential experiences; thus, appearing that the world is in a constant stage of change. In our world of misconstrued ideas and values; it seems we may be facing the reality of our own extinction. Without the awakening of our hearts and spirits, it seems we may be losing our race with humanity. The negative energy of greed, power and money is apparently occurring in every socialized grouping. Throughout millennia, we have finally arrived at the 21st-century in break neck speed. Now, I find myself at a loss in being able to accept the causation of such a cataclysmic decline in our world, and in the minds and hearts of those bent on destruction.

A CHOICE
In my mind, it seemed that my questioning God about so many things, was continually ongoing. Not only about the happenings within my own life, but other events in the world.

One cannot help but wonder why some are created to do havoc and evil while others are peacemakers and angelic in nature. Once again, I know the answer, CHOICES!

Knowing that my spirit is dwelling within this earthly form, gives me cause for reassessment. In the duplicity of the life cycle, brings about choices of good and bad. Realizing there are many of those whose choices of negative influences are introduced into our society every day. We are prompted through the effects of the media, Internet, and even to our interactions of others. Within these interconnections, we find ourselves being inundated by many untruths. Discernment and seeking truth are the tools that we must implement on our journey.

On this planet, earth; we have been given the gift of choice. Although, the state of carnality appears to be the preferred choice for most. As we struggle within our lives; and try to fulfill our desires, for the most part, lose focus on the will of God.

In consideration of the ever-changing elements of love and loss, while on this journey of life on earth; we look to our *beginnings*.... *God. God* our Creator. I believe there is nothing left to chance. Circumstances, events, and unexpected happenings seem to be delivered at our doorstep, at the most opportune time. Whatever ways we ingest and procure these two elements.... love and loss; it is not without intention of growth and development. Whether in the highest unbounded love or in the deepest sorrow of loss, there is the aspect of gain. Once again, we look to God for help and answers. Through God, all things are made possible. It is our recompense to have faith within ourselves, and believe.

OUR SURVIVAL

Now is the time for each one of us to make a difference; if we want our beautiful planet to survive. We must be conscientious not only to care for one another, but for the living planet also. The choices are ours, to make that beneficial choice not only for ourselves but for humanity.

All of us have certain paths in which we are following. Making choices good or bad depends upon our consciousness; but, it seems we don't have the bigger choices. For we know that God is in charge of everything, he knows everything, because he created everything. Therefore, our Creator has the finality of our very existence. For within each one of us there is a solution. As a creative being, God instilled in us the powers to overcome negativity; through the shear will of God's love and light.

We are blessed with a heart and a mind, it is up to us to use these gifts and manifest a different world from that of the past. It is time to balance and buffer this negativity with our inherent God-given indwelling spirit, and our unconditional love. Whereby, all Healing can begin.

"It is the Lord that goes before you.
He will be with you;
he will not fail you nor forsake you.
Do not fear or be dismayed."

DEUTERONOMY 31:8

Fifteen

"Heaven means to be one with God."

CONFUCIUS

FOOD FOR THOUGHT

"For ages, you have come and gone courting this delusion. For ages, you have run from the pain and forfeited the ecstasy. So, come, return to the root of the root of your own soul.

Although you appear in earthly form Your essence is pure Consciousness. You are the fearless guardian of Divine Light. So, come, return to the root of the root of your own soul.

When you lose all sense of self the bonds of a thousand chains will vanish. Lose yourself completely, Return to the root of the root of your own soul.

You descended from Adam, by the pure Word of God, but you turned your sight to the empty show of this world. Alas, how can you be satisfied with so little? So, come, return to the root of the root of your own soul.

Why are you so enchanted by this world when a mine of gold lies within you? Open your eyes and come --- Return to the root of the root of your own soul.

You were born from the rays of God's Majesty when the stars were in their perfect place. How long will you suffer from the blows of a nonexistent hand? So, come, return to the root of the root of your own soul.

You are a ruby encased in granite. How long will you deceive Us with this outer show? O friend, we can see the truth in your eyes! So, come, return to the root of the root of your own soul.

After one moment with that glorious Friend you became loving, radiant, and ecstatic. Your eyes were sweet and full of fire. Come, return to the root of the root of your own soul.

Shams-e Tabriz, the King of the Tavern has handed you an eternal cup, And God in all His glory is pouring the wine. So, come! Drink! Return to the root of the root of your own soul.

Soul of all souls, life of all life - you are That. Seen and unseen, moving and unmoving - you are That. The road that leads to the City is endless; Go without head and feet and you'll already be there. What else could you be? - you are That."

RUMI

"I searched for God among the Christians
and on the Cross and therein I found Him not.
I went into the ancient temples of idolatry;
no trace of Him was there.
I entered the mountain cave of Hira
and then went as far as Qandhar
but God I found not.
With set purpose, I fared to the summit of Mount Caucasus
and found there only 'anqa's habitation.
Then I directed my search to the Kaaba, the resort of old
and young;
God was not there even.
Turning to philosophy I inquired about him from ibn Sina
but found Him not within his range.
I fared then to the scene of the Prophet's experience of a
great divine manifestation only
a "two bow-lengths' distance from him"
but God was not there even in that exalted court.
Finally, I looked into my own heart
and there I saw Him; He was nowhere else."

RUMI

Pene Enochs

"OUT WITH THE OLD, ON TO OUR NEW BEGINNINGS"

Pene

He instructs us. "Do not be conformed to this world, this age, fashioned after and adapted to its external, superficial but be transformed, changed, by the entire renewal of your mind, by its new ideas, and its new attitudes, so that you may prove, for yourselves, what is good and acceptable and perfect will of God, even the thing which is good and acceptable and perfect in His sight for you."

ROMANS 12:2

A NEW DAY

"Come with me, let us journey together in one accord.
Let us face our fears together,
and then release them all to God.
May we become that which is within each one of us,
the essence of the living God.
Let us recognize within each one the power that
we were designed for.
Our spirit man desires freedom,
freedom from shackles of a third dimensional self.
Come, come with me,
let us enter into the heavenly light.
Let us return home."

PENE

www.ingramcontent.com/pod-product-compliance
Lightning Source LLC
Chambersburg PA
CBHW041621220426
43662CB00001B/10